TH

GRACE L. LOWTHIAN

KULVERT
NEWCASTLE UPON TYNE

THE AZYGOS WADE

OUTLAWS

BEAUTIFUL INSOMNIAC

CALIMINARIAN

IF THE WIND STOPPED

CORNER OF BLINK

OUTLAWS

UP REDHILLS

A house stands still in Durham
its layered bricks have cracked
permanently
straining out mortar residue
bonding tapestries- puss and goo,
eroding souls since the last time you peaked
through
        it doesn't kiss me
        it doesn't miss me
we hold each other tight
I guess it feels- right

OUTLAWS

Popping spots and Catholic schools
he said "why won't you tell me what
happened in the white house"
-

We ran away from the day
surviving off the land and 1-5-5/6-5r14 tyres
versions of creator driving draped walls
brute, windows in picture frames growing
thinner of ditch
-

Throating syrinx song
a manless disguise salutes blowed
familiarity, thoughts to the arbitrary,
speaking mutation,
half on itself, half onto me
-

Impermanent foliage, a black mist rolls vaga
gaps out,, drops into gear
to the leafing borderline, with awaits:
--/.]';,-a--.sporadic touch of hand

HAWKER'S HUT

What happens when you start to see
the earth's curvature on the sea?
grievous smiles start to appear

your barbiturate breath
collapsed into particles
and contaminated into me
I didn't ask for solutions
more a response.

CONSETT'S ELEGY

Her breath-
still haunts the front street

her gait-
remains in cracked paths

in the chimes of litter,
in the rays of digital billboards;

it crackles:
                    Laissez faire!

                            Laissez faire!

        it cackles:

                    Laissez faire!

                            Laissez faire!

LET'S GO SHOPPING

It did not shock
that skin could peel
squeals.

The women flutter past reflections
bound by fabric that is caught in the door
automatically assuming,
raised chins
raise the day.

The men have flattened all perfections,
only   add an   im
I have piled my sight
in stacks of veins
twitching days
are left so stale.

Truculent to these ceremonies
we would break the air   once more
and that dinged door
would throw-throw-throw
our souls onto sale   once more.

Ride the sedate wave
stains snarl-

            Let's
            go shopping!

BEAUTIFUL INSOMNIAC

PHASE I...
LIVING ROOM
ENQUIRIES

Fortify,   departed.

"That's quite a snare for a sensible man"
I said
he replied:
"You write like the doubled lives of
Victorian men"

.   .   .

I exposed my body to the
swoosh   that knocked at the fireplace,
then   the   wind   sickly   swooned
the   left   side   of my   rib-
cage
.

.

.

PHASE II...
STATE OF MIND,
STATE OF MINE

Last week,
I overdosed on coffee buzzes.

Last year,
I let myself get sexually assaulted.

This week,
I've been crawling up in corners,
hoping I'm not a mother.

Today,
I thought about you.

Two years ago,
I killed you.

Last week,
I became a beautiful insomniac.

Last year,
I wrote a letter I didn't send.

This week,
I've been crawling up in corners,
hoping I'm a mother.

Today,
I went to the cinema.

Two years ago,
I killed you...

...I close my eyes,
I'm with you.

PHASE III...
CLOSE BACK
ROUNDED VOWEL

in the casual hours and minutes past
                    I think about
why are spots called polka
and   h
why are lines called stripes   u
                 I think about   him   n
on the casual ceiling, hanged, turned to   g

--a,e,i,o,u

PHASE IIII...
MORI

Me and the birds have
thought about tying
our two arms, legs, wings, and feet;
so that when,
we fly, we fleet,
to an endless sleep
        and
what a tragedy the clouds will have to see

living their *intangible* existence emotion- free
they will now
realise
the sharp separations,, caused,,
by the aversus airplanes.

If the stiff mountain peaks replicated you or
the state,
would there ever be such a place for me to
escape?

PHASE ~~IIII~~... LINGERING I LYE

Lingering I lye
in alstroemerias maze
how a kiss can dye- in its darkness
asking for hand on heart.

              ?
Embark   !
twisting fibres
cottons turn to sand
scraping metals with chewed food
        duvets once radium
eyebrows radiate with a hollow glow.

Lingering hands constructing spider web
lies, mythically assuming its curl is a claw...
brain: b-beat, b-beat, b-beat, beats
with the calendar eagle bone
scratching out tallied days- plan in place
weave my fingers to your left breast plate...

The rhythm: Seamlessly dressed.

PHASE I̶H̶I̶ I...
TO RISE

When I wake up in five o' clock Ams
the day is already set, like a Roman plan.
In orifice, a baby tooth remaining,
conjectures, it is Christmas;
my attainted bruised eye, knows,, it is grief.
Mental melting
mortal moon, glows bones into calcium.
Transferring into dreams, she has raised me
dead, cloaked me, in her shedding tear.
Toes tip. Tipping round laws of an upstairs
neighbour: its bureaucracy alienates,
hatches out muted colours.
Mornings muzzle me from the flooding
dripped day,
I slip my actions onto pale china plates.

~ ~

When I go to sleep in five o' clock Ams
the dream?.. Already set to a hypnagogic
kaleidoscope chime.
Out-voyeur, a half orphaned pause, fading
ethereal, in eulogic law.
To panoptic gong pits...

Prophecies through
the proud pained dovecote-
draw long my straggled stray in rhizome.
Over the eye bagged shore to the field of
reeds,
these ways-filled of frailed hem chorus:
*

To rise, To rise...
Do we lumber -on-in- this eternal night?
To rise, To rise...
I've seen this life through mind tides~
To rise, To rise...
Just to lay in mutual bone medium,
by-a-side-
*

CALIMINARIAN

THE DENE

in the midgie dance
spearhead breathing branches
chariot to the first part of vaults;
Out/In all living convex
fly further and around
to keep us alive

WATERFALL, WATERFALL

Pregnant blossom sprinkles rain
over satellite-view hairies
parachute pecks land on liquid flow.

And the trials!
between sister quarries
hone the mechanical milked mill wheel.

Drown us in lullaby
mine us to sleep
         as the cradle known had no float
         we were heading towards sea.

Carried children, seeking constellation
in two thirds of Orion
two thirds of gorge
         we waterfall.

POKE

Preference, of round fingertips
sewing stars to the black
infinitesimal decorations
migrating through the psyche map.

On a Sunday, the clouds are etched blinds
puppet stringed on my patch of sky
seaweed amongst the grass stain
I just slither as a horizontal lie.

THE 4AM WORD

the thriving thought of him
ungloving the pulse of the 4 am word
under the tones of stained glass breathe
new patterns in meditation mind
new colours of starvation

slanted, dripped in dipping too
between the north east/and/south west
he dreams under the tickling trees
I dream from the clitoris

and the clitoris,
hanged like the dream catcher-
how this intimate morning, so bare in a quiet
existence, creams through the mandala,
out to the veined street

<-^***the sun gives birth to the new inwards
fade of blue***^->

and when the hinges of the lips screw onto
another's sea

I'll 'be thinking of you

IN-NO-THOUGHTS
OF THE FLOOD

diagonal-and
myopia dreams fistfight on pastures
pouring jostled commits of airborne
aggregates to still for the ruminate
village folk

rictus walled valleys strum daybreak
with no true heaven to roof their hope,
ironing 'what ifs' into front street
dodo scopes

to what a landlord subculture grows bricks
not crops- returned,
because everything has already happened:
I can't write in intercedes
         -every man I meet waters me down

*vague women feminine, true mystic of
creed, cast on visual thesis, extort realism to
a fizzed ransom love

AT THE SUNSET PUPPET SHOW

Sienna fell to cry on the hills,,
tinged all optics to the tentacle land
kids sat on broken hour, bending
picture books to pinhole sights

the afternoon cackled
as a drowned meat factory,
folds the soul amain
to a marked sketched spy
Sienna, days are sieved remains
scrying attics in the skull of time:

watching the dream leased through the roof
apparently it's the best view to see
when eternity springs on trampolines and
slits of virtue fall off youth's wing

the flirting floorboards fret this wrinkled
blood:
a purgatory model- to- a patio gesture,

beseeches a fenced tongue
glued to heal together with slava

in bitter dock promises
the myth of the velcro is lost,
Laurelle stands in crowds
leaking cavitated laughter

shadows walk off washing lines
         and
figures are saddled on intervals,
at the sunset puppet show.

TRYING TO GROW

Amongst stale byes
half a devotion retires
dripping alone on a platform joins
shady considerations

fire on a leash
poised in wry hickeys
complaints limage
into orgy

circulating red questions
eyes are but a nursery
this is the time of confer
into solar rent

elastic laughing marries
implicit paid waters
generator washing
our scattered coups.

He is hell my wild love,
lonely
in a trained "miss-ya".

Likable clay
sculptured state
blood paw printed on cheek
scissor chops fistula

spoiling the dishing out of the calf
trying to grow;
in a bannered
preferable way.

My stale sweats burn hickeys
       tonight~!
They rest in flemish chains.

TRUTH OF A SHADOW

Woman ----
        Fingers can not flicker
Woman ----
        Come on in under
Woman ----
        Flesh, it may wither
Yellow Woman ----
        Your flesh-in a gentle tether
Woman ----
        Bones do not bend forever
Women~~~
        Smoking so pleasantly behind
        their orange veils
        Machinery dance of fingers-stale
        so stale.

A laced cosmic colour only woven
from the dream, has created new substance,
on the paper, into tobacco brain.
Drips meow in purred jazz out the soul
chains. And the shadow in freak!
        The truth of the shadow in freak!
Black storm ash figurines
pointed dipped finger guns

attack- shot- base camp lungs.

Twitch twitch ---- The sundown knows.
Twitch twitch ---- The sundown moves:
                 rebounding declination of
                 crepuscular perfume.

Gabled clonks- the bells travel on silence's
loan, when days lie down in their two-toned
laws.

Strangles from withdrawal ventilations.
The opaque just dances, and does not pass
through-benedictions of:
The passage/The prism/My love/His love
\Our Love
Death: will find my life-
Naked...voided...
with enough ash
to blanket a home.

WHERE THE CATNIP GROWS

Whispering rain coats the viaductal heat
till moss develops an emberish rash,
a sailing sanctuary burns on the waxy Wear.

Sixteen sliced half bitten plates of flesh
arrested the air on suspicion of mute,
rent is just a hollow scatter in a dark matter,
and the latter just patter ha-ha
 when thoughts ask does he like ya'
– nah-ah!

Here the rifle range shoots abandonment
:
your kiss itself- a branding iron
smoke is the ghost of a heat's past:
a temporary lay of the hot air balloon head
tosses to turn, cradles in ash
now I diet from the sun
only the lagoon knows
I indulge in the moon
hypnotic beams in beating bud,,
missionary sirens squealing schemes,

in licentious ceremonies,
we gauge erect seamless sails in time for the
tempest.

***   ***   ***   ***   ***   ***   ***   ***

Sparkling stream
maligning machine
BARK! The dogmatic eels they sing
what sky anuses the intergalactic gateway
that leads true binaries brings?

Till thirteen crawling pythons
pretend they are our ciphers
and still the use of the wind is unknown

up sublimest scattered limestone lies
on the trance of sighs we float
into spired pyramids only tonight,,
the solemn bricks hide tickets in cracks
to jump and sink
into the gooey mute air..,,,,,

That ego eagle!
did you move each grain of soil with a flap?
do your words sizzle for a guaranteed grave?
Archaic wretch in the burning night!

Why do you sweat through the cloak of
armour in parade?

~~~~~~~~~~~~~~\\\~~~~~~~~~~~~~~

We whisper in raincoats under the viaduct,,,-
the heat, how you steam my howl
the filth, how do I thank your soul for
baptising my mind?
: You thumping thumping flesh,
when you moooooooooooove into twig:

the cool cats will lie, to lay,
within your nip.

LES MINCES

At the death postcode- an invisible gate-
where angelic hums guide
coming to this world in sighs.
~~~~~~~~~~~~~~~~~~~~~~~~~~~~~~~~~~~~~~~
Fountains have been wandering from
streams
beside canals I hum fresh studies!

Floury flesh, quivers amongst the perverted
desolate street,
cascade the dying lips with a smacking pipe

grailed bleach, sold in 24-hour pharmacies
preached over to present a thick wool snog
of 'dose'

enslaved in nocturnal dependency
you cellared their thirst into flexible foam

weeping astral in true. Colours tousled.
retreats in overnight lyres--/. Destroy myself

cats shed tears in cimetière du père-lachaise
they don't do it for the people you know

THE FLOWERS!
THE NIGHT!

shadowing cypresses
strolling on the night
smoking against the flowers

lucid bird flaps
clipping the wing of our days
songs drip mortal

when the dusk-mid staggers
awoken phone calls
into tired forgetful blossomless mornings

such regime
frothing to kelp
recalling their existence amongst

IF THE WIND STOPPED

EASY ON THE EYE

...and what remains
but blue tack stretch marks on the wall

cigarette ash freckles
two-day old tea

my dark room fingering
the street of artificial sun pockets

below the red houses of Heaton transmuting
the morning, collapsing to the nautical

they observe in eclipse
at my emerging bone hand

drooped in cling
out the crocodile window

slithers of the 'ing' wind
remaining on

But! A train ridden inferno, fuelled by the
micro fire of yazoot breathing

~~*~~*~~*~~*~~*~~*~~*~~*~~*~~*~~*
/\

In the waking sleep
theremins below weep up wells
squirming in faint ears ,,, "I feel like dust".

A place unknown | has stolen me in sleep
I tomb marathons| in soil

and I'm just wearing hands.

HIGH FRIAR LANE

Shrieked slain sins
hailing to the sick daytime star,
perced a-new
on the lane-less hoarded sky

before the gazed caned capture
crossed in clique as the sheaf,
revolvers at the last order chime
sprint thrums round the legs of another seat

rare off-sloped blithe rely
travelling in visual ill to watery cheeks,
the etch of a shoe sole steps away
before you do
how the thought of her sticks figured eights
round ya teeth

WHILE I WRITE
ON MY LUNG

While I write on my lung- I do not believe
my smoke is determined by my roll- it has
submissively cascaded under the
dictatorship of clippers.

Maybe all my thoughts come from my lung
as I try and reach to another sun [blue star]
I'm sat where you are, and where you
were——

——stop the trilithon search, you know it is
here, your massaged palms, they tell you so
in chokes
——-don't sing to me like that, star blue, I'm
crying cause I love
————-----you, you proclaiming to my street: I
am a part of your life, don't disappoint them
now.— the sky is walking and crawling and
mourning into morning, and they have
started to question our drugs, and our love,
                you know lust is outdated now
                        in the shadow of your smile.

They have started to question our drugs to
the point of our existence—— but we are
not addicted, Ginsberg said so
—-most times, sometimes, I see him under
his rose like a bumble sucking on blossom,
she is always with him—- how could I see
that in this cancerous world
—— so he sticks his democratic chin up, all
skeleton trees wave~~~by the metro
————- there is nothing, and he is worth
more than this 6 pound system—-
the holy trinity of
——ego——-greed-———-lust——
easily translated,   HOLY, through the star
blue equation:
——dharma——God——baphomet
!
You're gently far away into the tonight
my love
while you write on my lung
is it lust or just love suicide-ing our
friendship.
~While I write on your lung
'What breathes'
?

HIDING PLACE

Coat hangered dreams kept scents
ironed- choiced- wardrobed|--|
from the messy corner creased day.
Tobacco sprinkled splinters
reaching out- silver harmonic handles,.
Haloed
spit burns of E and A

memories of locker-ed welt
jagged succession of meaded jaw
orbital hieroglyphs parch healing
at rate concession, her values light raw,.
Passaging

ripped red empire grids
bloom from rights of sugar pot hibernation,
till the May flowers are stirring flavours:
notes of granulated addiction, ribbon stick
aura dusts poised gilt visions

the mourned after-glow-s-dim from his
finger picking scribbles
mirrored radiance;
on fretted mind- the auditory!

Twisting-to-witness
clouds receipt;
the bones of her song.
Drench ~ Desolate
on the other side of this blistered boist azure.

PRONOUNCED FRIENDSHIP

Elm, the cobble curls marble
calm carpet——cooperate the storm that
basements
my eyes

this hideous summer bowled on chosen
flowers
name the tiger that roams these new times
home

lay lay with the slab of this earth
concrete agonise lymphatic laboratory
poppy seeds

mechanic conversations with corpses
they pronounce me dead- a cigarette
but~bum

angels in the flicker of a rolling skin
congregate clysmic requiem
amen

pissed by thy rain
I knock on Anglican doors begging the
world for
forgiveness
——I'm so sure it's not me who needs it

west elation puss-ing a double bed mattress
to the glands of the street, the sign of a
post- industrial
spring

noises between thunder
clung sways of metronome hearts,
jailing ravished paths
alone.

WHEN THE FLAME'S BLUE

The great verve
of errand music;
if you looked in the mirror with me
side by side
crying petals
from soil eyes
bleeding empty into another life

the rain reminds in sleep when up
coming down in smoked to the bone
brief room
I evaporate broth-like
when the flame's blue

where do all the colours go, in our
in-betweens
of rattles with sound- burning plastic
crunched in overcrowded droop
you treat me as chore.

Revising the patterns of euros
in the gas collar:
when you try to catch my
pomegranate paint, to light us alive
from the embrace of a keyhole
echo-chambered,
bed~bugging on hum.

==*
|
|

U?nder this street light false star,

The blaze blues*
*

where are   ...you*
where you   ... are

NEW INFANCY
OF FUNERAL

As when a new death is begun——since
teenage attempts——the roof of our
twenties head——
seek in the end,,, floated credits—— enter
through their remembrance——
new infancy of funeral——
clashed flesh~utters—— to! A lean
heaven risen—— enter through plethora-ing
romances——
retired empty full wheel—— spinned
sentient slava——enigmatic thread in peels
to beams—— of adverts on gallows——
enter ancient——'trip with trembled
goodbye'——vacuums of this town in tinned
fire——reap her malted brine into soda——
it was always pussing powder*** that sought
the end of you—— from a few mutters of
law—— his dusty daughter of grimaced
masculine confusion—— lips beneath
length—— renting a smile un-perished

——I stink in its grief.
I stink of grief——

IF THE WIND STOPPED

~~~~~~~~~~~~~~~~~~~~~~~~~~~~~~~~~~

Narrow thought jungles swing from
the vista sienna brick of Heaton creaks,
some parakeets hum in cheap poetic beats
on the high street,
some lianas lose their crawl trying to
trumpet English veins,
those poor trees, right-, trunked with a red
blood filter, existing in an azonic narcotic
side- streaming smoke.
~~ *

    *

      *

Oxygenic broke—I start to dream in shades
of sepia sludge, tarantula-ing through blue
lives and floorboards that cleave even the
nano-est of DVD indents, pitted with the
traumas of childhood. —No polycarbonate
plastic base can stonewall death tourists—

in the days of the dog star
I truly was rebirthed in the bladder of the

catacombs.
Soundtracked by the sorcery of the last
heartbeat of hawkers hut
fourteenth July twenty twenty one.
It all colonnades—in faint bone beige tender
soot— at a place unknown.

/In conduit flow, through a pipeline
major~minor pattern of flute/

~~~

there's BABY.WASP rulers —stinging ya
sing—flying round the dumb earth façade to
guard their magnitudinal USB core.
—Walking down Shieldfield and there's
empty baby prams growing out the grass like
flowers—common condom packet garden
weed killer—seaweed skyscrapers swaying
sloppy like my blinking polyommatus Icarus
eyes — clouds picnicking over spired roofs—
in canopy, my feet ripped the epipelagic
zone, flying up-down the thermocline...
To the corner-less mystery of the mind—

~~~

regolith- mars oxide dust eclipses in
poking thaw,

in the cracked up pavements—where you
used to slide;
the sun's umbra in the night has shown
arcane territory,
~do not collate us to a white noise lamp post,
even if you want to~

I hated puberty
and in my polytechnic days, I was still in a
puberty grass stain.
~*My body in entablature—/Anno
Domini/—and all other things that didn't
last*~
Neptune tiding , broken beaches, vulgaris,
meant broken waves
:   in every stage, the cliff became his.
This'll come a tragedy
take   to   play   amongst
some   nettles   you
lay
time upwhirls underworld
flames.

Back
To
Stomach
Head   To   Toe

over you, flesh will turn   compost
so that you will grow,
so that we are one,
so that we'll photosynthesise,
or so that we'll meet in landfill scum...
to only
tumble in travel;
over broken beaches
and be due
on the broken *sands, of the
broken   *
waves.   *
~~~~)~~~~

Not much is happening past Cardigan
Terrace on a Tuesday:
in the tick of the Anthropocene,
liquorice papers burn.
/

Jitterbug desert shiver— cacti at the door,
looking like a yawn—
are you shaking the spear? Are you
sweeping up the wind?
But a time not to fly... What is the rain to the
butterfly?
What is the waking dream? A time for sight
to flutter in limp on swollen blight skies?
Could a Mandala of words un-line to save

to flutter in limp on swollen blight skies?
could a mandala of words un-line to save our
unborn generation?
the unborn-unlined -too lined- generation,
smoking in streams of
blue, all my poems are written by the
kitchen door, do they ever mosey off the fire
escape in search of the sirocco...
)
when it gets past 4... !oh my love, oh my life!
we are never
awake for the great gasp of the sky.
~~~~~~~

The meaning lays in the colluding
calaminarian meadow of the subconscious...
it's swaying with the return of spring...
conflations are what the dark matter solace
brings to its bathing stars...
~~~~~

if the wind stopped,

—

you would be everywhere tonight.

MOUNTAIN CALLED MASTURBATE

In a sluttish temple, you have gained
full membership to rim the room.
Unfolding corners derange oblivion deeds.
Fountains of thirst, carpets of blonde human
hair: this mocking fashion of appetite has
learnt the strokes of your patterned brain;
the lack of keys, the lack of light,
hides you in the walls of the cream pain that
paints "Where did the rash go"?
The pillar that moans to the ceiling cries:
"The world rash is in debt to the rotten
rent of healing. Out there, life is melting, in
here...
  You might as well finish".

CORNER OF BLINK

MESH GRINS, IN RECLUSION

There's a street between the breath of -----
succumb
                        splitting, and fabled
gambles
                                learning the sappys
                                through each slot
pusher penny;

                                early- demos
                                late- conforms
                                                half
bitten
                                archived in mania
there's a loose thread that scrawls off-the
valance of its sky.

MONOPHONIC

only you flow
and only we've met
in dissipations

only I lock
and only we're open
in burglar-ations

what chant do we believe in,
when we come together?

in this cell- once bunker
nothing, and no devotion

only we gagged
and only the drool graffities,
in reclamations

Gospel islands effluence
from man-made England

THE RUNGS

we are all burps
of the angel   gurgling down
        streets of flagellation
we stumble home
        but! take the scenic route
by alimentary canals
        we walk with such pace
our ankles fluke
we are   running away
        from something

        we probably are.

TREWHITT RD.

Blotting the circumcised day, baby
kicks of the winter clats, exhorting
tears I could never cry, umbilical
cords laugh wraps to flapped fan gaps,
holding microphones up to signal.

It's a thousand bins fallin over on the
backstreet tradesmen install the limbo
line, they've watched me sleep and they've
watched me wake, they've been the
rustling tin bent back into shape.

Still, here with me
moving, not,
when gulls drop off my filler words, dunking
cigarettes in coffee seas to get an extra hit of
life, students are putting a year of their lives
in a bin, after the council has dossed the
rounds, so breakers can shine on
one last foreskinned day.

Bathed in carpet burn:
violent shimmies of the metro soundtrack
the black dust

who the force?
just the force...
...who forces
        itself into bland grooves of sky.

UNCANNY W.

Walls seldom of colour
ruefully boil plain reds
is it lids who hold prolific pupils?
or the new rouge whose vigour's the sign of
          NO BALL GAMES.

A wagging Warhol army
repeating and repeating
not soup today for breakfast *like*
just jam-ed, bubbling on the stove
of their blinkish war
they're creased.

Everyone I know a grain on my wall,
watching me cheat on myself
watching me and my pathetic pants.

TODAY

Realising we are no good for each other
-beings-
caged lions that consume and costume,
in morning concrete
comedown- clay, drooped in flesh ready for
the next mould.
Melting down molten wrought fire escapes,
fusing we are walking adverts
for the design of death
                    promised wash of
endometrium- summers,
as a thin line of froth dissolves
on a shit poured pint
letters downing-one way-
dragging them through white splinters of
February's brown eyes-the other-
caught back by rubato, only cause our
jackets said so
slammed gate- lulls
zipping rosy cheeks out the back door,
to what I couldn't say.

RELAY

The future dimmed into 1834's falling
mezzotint depiction of Babylon
white hurls chalked the knurls of time
with the last and no religion
arrows dragged to their bowed grip of
cumulonimbus
already- conjured in its own exploded guilt
of assembly
arms position to a new light
fingers scream to a virgin cloud

      :

neoteric instruments of zephyr
convoluted on extensions from the
Rube Goldberg machine
wails between this strum in the meagre
abode
runs the arrows rapture, reckoning
through centuries of stairwayed
grease spits and ice cream van man tuning
the house of the sky is empty
as free as the folks not at home
so we run\down raptures the arrow ponders
in some rude passage of silence
the personification of W's, L's, T's and O's

flap false around this sprint
don't forget to feed the babies plasma;
crawling in distillations on slurped shadow
shavings
into its filth,
between the relay of the crude door.

UNDER-CLOUD

A place stolen in sleep
crowded chatters/powdered privileged
bone nose
noisy names- never heard
a mattress with no frame
no flame, groans>>> perfect frequency
unearthing the voices from
the obelisk head
never serenading the stroke of sleep
but a place-in-sleep, and I'm in:.
worlds of Crown Posada tiled skies
margined streets unfolding like
threefold leaflets
Hell is not red, it's blank
and you're at the end of it,
pretending to be a stumble
of a strangers hand, running over
the beat of tapping fingers.

-A few murmurs of the sun-the moon
thumps black walls- never meeting the burn-

ABOUT A GIRL

In the grip of the bar mat.
-

She exits outside
the leather skin of that night
too far
moonshine ears fit the hiatus hat
karaoke loused up a tannery of flirts
too early
only remembering you
by the back of your empty head.

VACUUM

whole world moves
in a shiver
duality froths
shoulder padding each next-to's
of moon
fireworks choke, off the thrown butt:
spark tactisms

think of the sky's ceiling,
with nothing at all

last week on the bone train
doe's explicits, carriage off
the allude of fleets, the lucent admirers ogle
passing twice on the food trolley
evasive Zig / \ Zag love riding it's own
mobbed roding,
through washing machine kisses
everything turns and our tissue: sogged-
crumble
's of acne
brisket in the pocket of life's urn

think of the earth's carpet,
with everything and more

terrestrial currents
strip out the summer glove

withering the buttoned petals hostage
their winter full time show
sold out to the toured buckarooing
strand of hair

think on a chair of institution
with ciphered letters transcribed to
grocery receipts

HITCH-UALITY

Little silver spoon,
indecent on the mis-match saucer
consorting stirs
resting on the shelf of breasts
bouncing off each one~ a kid in a car
^   ^   ^

                              lamp

post   hopping

exiled in loose scaffolds
down waterslide pipes.

O' then,, we're caryatid rubble
in capitol of him.

TWIST-A-BROWN
DRYING

The clouds are collapsing their verse
who is their singer? Who is their painter?
        Manic
blue split ends of sky
withdrawing the carried backpack of space.
There are rolling figures
in the corners of my eyes.
One day they'll catch up with me soon.

SCARECROW STANDARDS ON DRIFT

Heap historical torso hills
latching shadows of the inside boy posture
and here you have poured standards of
infinity
caressing blue thoughts and blue walks,
back to a purple heathered home
all once tiny rope
6 papers left for the week, then we're
morning runners
here he folds postures of the inside crow
panther-ing the ink, pacing like an elbow
            writing
with his blackberry thorn arm
falling down miserable suburban streets,
leaking over a cotton Mrs.
-A whispering dialect ear poking
transmission

the stooge on the stooled Jupiter day
stimulant of the sky
the wind is snarling! Awake.

Have you heard of such endurance to the
bare acoustic seagull song?
When he evicts the hark of gated lobes
I am the fruit fly hovering on the vitamin of
your unripe breath.
One mention of my name lost in the
property of our rusting liver
the answer he wrote in my notebook:

                    /

tranSITORY/
FREEDOM
NO\ CHAINS
        \

        a whispering dialect ear poking waxed
omission

now show my hand, the one who tattoos
carbon hearts in palms,
the handles of the bier;
through revivals of dug mastaba
mind burrows.
Endless! Endless! Beat on the drift
it's probably a glass forest, sanitised
by vicious fathers, gurning the grave.
                    Fuck the limit
Everybody's dead! In the cupboard of the
future who sneaks out the present

to mosh pit on the tide of receding hairs
yet goosing through shaves.
-A whispering dialect...
my ears could love you   /
but
theres probably a glass forest sharding
in his head.

DOODLES ON A FRIDGE LAMENT FROM STALE MAGNETS

Estranged Mother
Dead Daddy,

I hide my weeps in latent trees
do you hear them hunch
in the winter breeze?
When the sun's affair is burning!
BURNING! Baby fat
out my spanked face.

Love is legal legislature,
hiding leisure in picnic hipflask hobbies
pegged in poured grip of mud trail seeks
bubbling spilt-- sipping just
sticky sapping lard.

The bats hold me more
when tea is called.

CRUCI MUTE CANDESCENT

-Where your sound holed me an after-
                    !Bildung   !Bildung
whored wade on shadowy origin,
loose loins- becoming- ridge outmode

pressures collapse infantile, pouring inverts
off skin; radge ascent of
bruised mornings, priming winter contours
misprisoned bone,
three storied under cheek/

landscapes implode ticks-
itself a knotted room,
murderess chipping sky,
open on contingent spill

slipped figurations dance the throttled fell
all once fixus,
she skips into ends.
Decrying – Distance

UNDERSTANDING PATHOS

-On the down we are making where we meet
a gleam of stinks~already been
the guest who cleans for tomorrow's cleaner
the air that dilates the sky square dry
the sun masquerading as the moon
strange torture- evening classes of day
in the chalkboard surface of chasm thigh
volcanic valleys spit out mirrors: FAIL

*

I miss the feeling of familiar crows
pecking the screws at the fence of my bones
each footstep rustles wonder into a squished
electric burp
hoping to hop scotch your heart from
northern brickwork
so used eugeroic left us to revolt on Lim
searching rang after another's splattered
fetch
hence
the citadel cheers dim

ACKNOWLEDGMENTS

'Cruci Mute Candescent' was previously published by Kulvert as part of the Underground River #5 broadsheet in 2024.

OTHER BOOKS BY KULVERT

AVAILABLE FROM KULVERTBOOKS.COM
AND ALL GOOD BOOKSHOPS.

Special thanks to Koef Nielsen for all of the advice and support that made this book possible.

Cover photograph by the author.

First published in Great Britain
January 2025 by Kulvert.

ISBN 978 1 0685200 6 8

Ten copies signed and numbered by the author.
First Edition KV-008

This book is printed entirely on recycled paper.

kulvertbooks.com